Hands-On Science

Science Fair Projects About Weather

ROBERT GARDNER

D1200783

Enslow Publishing
101 W. 23rd Street
Suite 240
New York, NY 10011
USA

enslow.com

Published in 2017 by Enslow Publishing, LLC.
101 W. 23rd Street, Suite 240, New York, NY 10011

Library of Congress Cataloging-in-Publication Data
Names: Gardner, Robert, 1929-
Title: Science fair projects about weather / Robert Gardner.
Description: New York, NY : Enslow Publishing, 2017. | Series: Hands-on science | Audience: Age 8-up. | Audience: Grade 4 to 6. | Includes bibliographical references and index.
Identifiers: LCCN 2016019997| ISBN 9780766082069 (library bound) | ISBN 9780766082045 (pbk.) | ISBN 9780766082052 (6-pack)
Subjects: LCSH: Weather—Experiments—Juvenile literature. | Science projects—Juvenile literature.
Classification: LCC QC981.3 .G3795 2017 | DDC 551.5078—dc23
LC record available at https://lccn.loc.gov/2016019997

Printed in China

To Our Readers: We have done our best to make sure all websites in this book were active and appropriate when we went to press. However, the author and the publisher have no control over and assume no liability for the material available on those websites or on any websites they may link to. Any comments or suggestions can be sent by e-mail to customerservice@enslow.com.

Portions of this book originally appeared in the book *Wild Science Projects About Earth's Weather* by Robert Gardner.

Photo Credits: Cover, p. 1 prudkov/Shutterstock.com (lightning); Sunny Forest/Shutterstock.com (clouds on back cover); Strejman/Shutterstock.com (handprint on spine); design elements throughout book: ctrlaplus/Shutterstock.com (quote bubbles), Bimbim/Shutterstock.com (science doodles in blue background), Sergey Nivens/Shutterstock.com (lightbulb), Paul Velgos/Shutterstock.com (notebook), StepanPopov/Shutterstock.com (question marks); p. 4 24Novembers/Shutterstock.com.

Illustrations by Joseph Hill

Contents

Introduction

Weather depends on many things—the temperature of the air, the time of year, the amount of water in the air, and more. In this book, you will learn about weather by doing experiments. You will measure temperature, air pressure, and rainfall. You will even make it rain in your kitchen. You will see how temperature changes with location, time of day, and season. Experimenting will help you understand air pressure, clouds, how clouds form, and some of the other forces that affect our weather.

Entering a Science Fair

Most of the experiments in this book have ideas for science fair projects. However, judges at science fairs like experiments that are creative, so do not simply copy an experiment from this book. Expand on one of the ideas suggested or develop a project of your own. Choose something you really like and want to know more about. It will be more interesting to you. And it can lead to a creative experiment that you plan and carry out.

Before entering a science fair, read one or more of the books listed under Further Reading. They will give you helpful hints and lots of useful information about science fairs.

Safety First

To do experiments safely, always follow these rules:

1 Always do experiments **under adult supervision**.

2 Read all instructions carefully. If you have questions, **check with the adult**.

3 Be serious when experimenting. Fooling around can be dangerous to you and to others.

4 Keep the area where you work clean and organized. When you have finished, clean up and put all of your materials away.

5 When doing these experiments, use only non-mercury thermometers, such as those filled with alcohol. The liquid in some thermometers is mercury. It is dangerous to breathe mercury vapor. If you have mercury thermometers, **ask an adult** to take them to a local mercury thermometer exchange location.

Sun and Shade

Things You Will Need:

- bright, sunny day
- sheet of cardboard
- outdoor thermometer
- dry grassy place in sunlight
- dry grassy place in shade
- pencil
- paper

On a sunny day, where does it feel hotter: in sunlight or in shade? Write down your ideas and your reasons for them.

Let's Investigate!

1 Do this experiment on a bright, sunny day. Put a sheet of cardboard on dry ground where the sun can shine on it. Read the air temperature on an outdoor thermometer. Write down that temperature on a piece of paper.

2 Put the thermometer on the cardboard. Watch the thermometer until the temperature stops changing. Then write the temperature on the paper.

3 Move the cardboard and the thermometer. Put them on dry ground that is in shade.

4 Watch the thermometer until the temperature stops changing. Then write the temperature on the paper.

Is the temperature in the shade different from the temperature in sunlight? If it is, where is the temperature higher?

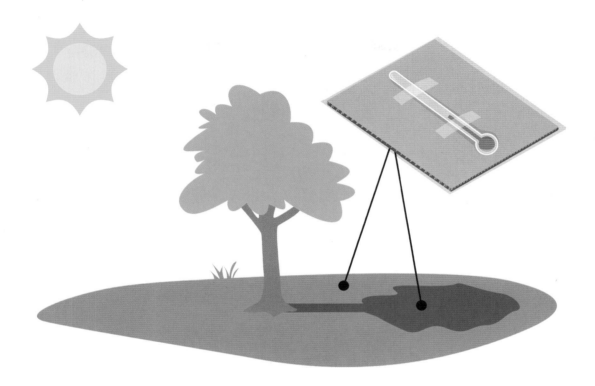

Sun and Shade: *The Facts*

The sun is a very hot place. The temperature at the sun's surface is about 6,000 degrees Celsius (11,000 degrees Fahrenheit). That's about 200 to 300 times hotter than Earth's surface. Energy from the sun heats Earth's air. Your thermometer measured the temperature of the air. There is less sunlight in shade. The object making the shade has soaked up or reflected a lot of the sun's light and heat. As a result, temperatures in shade are less than temperatures in sunlight.

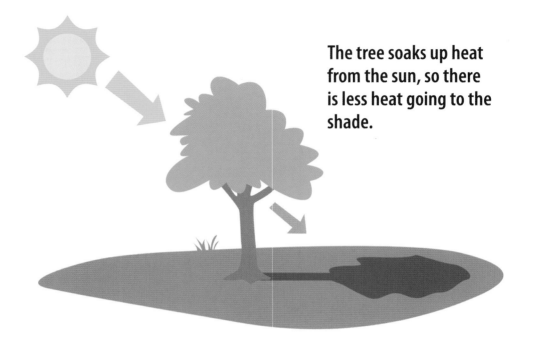

The tree soaks up heat from the sun, so there is less heat going to the shade.

Ideas for Your Science Fair

- In the experiment, you put the thermometer on dry ground. Would the temperature be different if the thermometer bulb is wet? If so, why?

- Is the temperature under the ground different from the temperature on the ground? Do an experiment to find out.

- Which side of a building (east, west, north, or south) is the coolest at different times of the day? Do experiments to find out.

2

Follow the Temperature All Day

Things You Will Need:

- sunny day
- thermometer
- shade
- clock or watch
- paper and pencil
- cloudy and rainy days

On a sunny day, when do you think the temperature will be highest? Morning? Noon? Afternoon? Write down your ideas and your reasons for them.

Let's Investigate!

1 Start this experiment early in the morning on a sunny day. Put an outdoor thermometer in a place where it will be in shade all day. Under a bush close to the house is a good place.

2 Look at the thermometer every hour or more often. Do this until after sunset. Each time you look, write down the temperature. Make a record like the one shown in the drawing on the next page. At what time was the temperature highest? Lowest?

3 Repeat this experiment on cloudy and rainy days as well as on other sunny days. Do your results vary?

Follow the Temperature All Day: The Facts

When your location on Earth gets more heat than it loses, the air temperature rises. On most days, Earth gets more heat from the sun than it loses, until the middle of the afternoon. As a result, the temperature keeps rising until some time between 2 p.m. and 4 p.m. The sun gives Earth the most heat in the middle of the day (around noon). This is when the sun is highest in the sky. It continues to give more heat than is lost until the middle of the afternoon.

What might cause the highest temperature to occur at a different time?

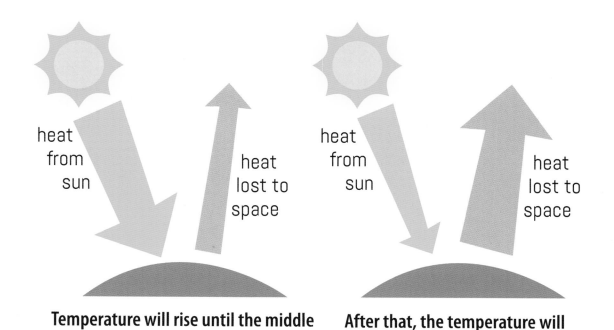

Temperature will rise until the middle of the afternoon.

After that, the temperature will fall.

Ideas for Your Science Fair

- **Let water flowing into a can represent heat from the sun. Let water flowing out of a hole in the can represent heat lost to space. Use this model to illustrate highest daytime temperature.**

- **On which side of a house (north, south, east, or west) is the air temperature highest? Does it depend on the time of day?**

3

The Changing Seasons

Things You Will Need:

- sheet of paper
- table
- dark room
- flashlight
- globe

Why is it colder in winter than in summer? Write down your ideas and your reasons for them.

Let's Investigate!

1 Put a sheet of paper on a table in a dark room. The paper represents part of Earth's surface. A flashlight represents the sun. Shine the flashlight straight down onto the paper.

2 With the flashlight at the same distance from the paper, tip it so its light hits the paper at an angle. What happens to the amount of surface covered by the light? In which case (1 or 2) would the sun give Earth more heat?

3 Put a globe on a table in a dark room. Find the Tropic of Capricorn on the globe. On the first day of our winter, the sun shines directly on the Tropic of Capricorn. Shine the flashlight straight on the globe's Tropic of Capricorn.

4 Slowly move the flashlight upward, but keep it parallel to the floor. All light rays from the sun that reach Earth travel side by side. Stop when the light shines on the United States. Does the light now cover more surface than it did when it shone on the Tropic of Capricorn? Why will it be colder in the United States than in countries farther south?

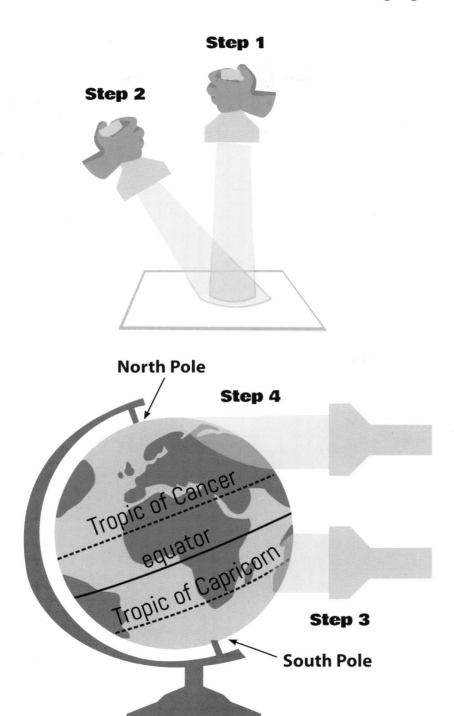

Step 1

Step 2

North Pole

Step 4

Tropic of Cancer

equator

Tropic of Capricorn

Step 3

South Pole

The Changing Seasons: *The Facts*

Is winter colder because Earth is farther from the sun? No! Earth is actually closer to the sun in January than in July. But Earth is tilted. That is why a globe on a stand is tilted. Light from the sun shines directly on the Tropic of Capricorn on December 21. But farther north, sunlight hits Earth at an angle. The light is more spread out. You discovered this when shining the flashlight on the globe. The heat from North America's winter sun is more spread out. Less heat is given to each acre of land so it is colder. Seasons happen because Earth is tilted.

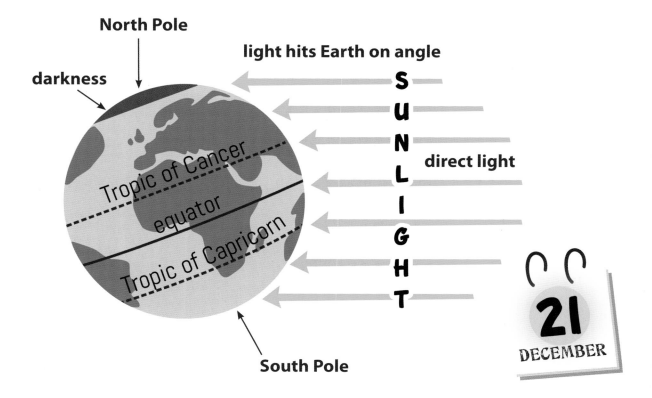

Ideas for Your Science Fair

- Use a globe and a lightbulb to show that the North Pole has 24 hours of sunlight during summer in North America.

- Light hitting at an angle gives less heat than light shining straight on something. Do an experiment to show that this is true.

4

The Air We Breathe

Weather—rain, snow, sleet, clouds, sunshine—happens in the air that surrounds us. What do you think air is? Write down your ideas and your reasons for them.

Let's Investigate!

1 Put a folded paper towel in the bottom of a drinking glass. Turn the glass upside down. The towel should not fall out.

2 Put a deep dishpan in a sink. Fill the pan with water. Push the upside-down glass to the bottom of the dishpan. Does water go into the glass?

3 Keep the glass perfectly straight and lift it straight out of the water. Dry your hands. Remove the paper towel. Is the towel still dry? What does this tell you about air?

4 Turn the empty drinking glass upside-down. Push it down into the dishpan filled with water. Then turn it sideways under the water. What happens? Was it really empty?

5 Put a pint jar into the dishpan. Fill it with water. Have someone hold the water-filled jar's open end under the water as shown on the next page. Push an empty upside-down drinking glass into the pan. Tip the empty glass under the jar. Let the air bubbles go into the upside-down jar. What happens?

air

The Air We Breathe: *The Facts*

The towel stayed dry. Water did not enter the glass because it was filled with air. Air is a gas. It takes up space even if you can't see it.

When you turned the glass sideways under the water, bubbles of air came out. The glass was not really empty! It had air in it. You were able to collect the air. You let it bubble

wood

water

into the pint jar filled with water. The air bubbled up to the top of the jar. Air, like a block of wood, floats on water. The air collected at the top of the jar. It took up space and pushed the water out the bottom of the jar.

5

What Is Air Pressure?

Things You Will Need:

- an adult
- empty 1-gallon metal can with screw cap that used to contain cooking oil (Never use a can that had contained paint thinner or alcohol)
- water
- stove
- oven mitt
- thick piece of cardboard
- aneroid barometer
- tall building
- notebook
- pen or pencil

Do you think air can push on things? Write down your ideas and your reasons for them.

Let's Investigate!

1 Find an empty 1-gallon metal can with a screw cap. Wash the can thoroughly with dishwashing detergent and water. Rinse several times. This will remove any oil that might be left in the can.

2 Pour 1 cup of water into the can. **Ask an adult** to heat the can on a stove. Let the water boil for about three minutes. Steam will push the air out of the can.

3 **Ask the adult** to put on an oven mitt and *quickly* move the can to a thick piece of cardboard. Have **the adult** *immediately* seal the can with the screw cap. Watch the can slowly cave in. How can you explain what happens to the can?

4 **Have an adult** show you how an aneroid barometer measures air pressure.

5 **With an adult**, take an aneroid barometer inside a tall building. Measure the air pressure on the bottom floor and on the top floor. Why is air pressure less on the top floor?

6 Keep a record of the weather and barometer readings for several weeks. How can a barometer help you predict weather?

What Is Air Pressure? *The Facts*

Because air has weight, it pushes on everything. Steam pushed air out of the can. When the can was sealed, the steam cooled. It changed back to water. But air could not get back in. This meant there was very little air inside the can. The air outside pushed the can in.

Air pressure is less as you go higher. Why? Because there is less air to push on things.

Moist air weighs less than dry air, so its pressure is less. A drop in air pressure often means that rain or snow is coming. Increasing air pressure usually comes with fair weather.

The push from air outside the can is greater than the push from the little bit of air inside.

Ideas for Your Science Fair

- **Put an aneroid barometer in a clear plastic bag. Seal the bag.** With an adult's help, **use the sealed barometer to show how depth of water affects pressure.**

- **Make a device to show changes in air pressure.**

6

What Makes the Wind Blow?

Things You Will Need:

- balloon
- bicycle tire pump
- wind

Where does wind come from? Write down your ideas and your reasons for them.

1. Fill a balloon with air. The balloon squeezes the air inside it. This makes the air pressure inside the balloon bigger than the pressure outside.

2. Hold the mouth of the balloon next to your face. Slowly let the air out of the balloon. Can you feel the air blowing on your face? You have made a small wind.

3. Hold the end of the hose of a bicycle tire pump near your cheek. Slowly push down on the pump handle. This increases the air pressure inside the pump. Can you feel a wind blowing on your cheek? Now, what do you think causes the wind to blow?

4. Go outside when there is a wind. Wet your finger. Hold that finger up in the air. Which side of your finger feels coolest? That side is the direction from which the wind is blowing. Why do you think the windy side of your finger feels cool?

What Makes the Wind Blow?
The Facts

Wind is moving air. You found air moved out of the balloon and out of the pump. Air moves from higher air pressure to lower air pressure.

The wind made your finger feel cool. It was coolest on the side facing the wind. The wind made the water on your finger evaporate (change to a gas) faster. Evaporation makes the water that is left cooler.

If you have a weather vane, it will point toward the wind. The direction of the wind is the direction from which the air is coming. A west wind comes from the west.

A weather vane points in the direction of the wind and greater air pressure.

Ideas for Your Science Fair

- Build a wind (weather) vane that will point to the direction of the wind.
- Build a device to measure the wind's speed.
- Do an experiment to show that evaporation makes water cooler.

7

Rain from the Sky

Things You Will Need:

- small aluminum pie pan
- ice cubes
- large (1-quart) clear glass jar
- hot water

What makes it rain? Write down your ideas and your reasons for them.

1 Fill a small aluminum pie pan with ice cubes.

2 Add hot water to a clear glass jar until it is about two-thirds full.

3 Put the pan of ice cubes on the open top of the glass jar.

4 After about 15 minutes, look at the inside sides of the jar. What do you see?

5 Watch carefully for a few minutes. You may see drops of "rain" from the bottom of the pan fall into the jar. Or you may see drops of "rain" from the pan run down the side of the jar.

6 Carefully lift the pan of ice. What do you see on the bottom of the pan? How can you explain what you have seen? Where else have you seen something like this? How is your experiment similar to the way real rain is made?

aluminum pan

hot water

Rain from the Sky: *The Facts*

Some of the hot water in the jar changed to a gas.
We say it evaporated. Water that is a gas is called water vapor.
When the water vapor touched the cold pan, it condensed
(changed back to a liquid). The condensed water formed
drops. Some drops became so big they fell back into the jar.
This is similar to what happens in clouds. Clouds are many
tiny water drops. The drops form when water vapor cools and
condenses. If the drops grow big, they may fall as rain.

water vapor condenses water drops clouds

8

How Much Rain Has Fallen?

Things You Will Need:

- tall jar with straight sides such as an olive jar
- masking tape
- ruler
- marking pen
- open space outside
- stake
- paper
- pen or pencil
- local newspaper's weather section

How can rainfall be measured? Write down your ideas and your reasons for them.

Let's Investigate!

1 Find a tall jar with straight sides. Tape a strip of masking tape vertically to the outside of the jar.

2 Using a ruler and a marking pen, make marks at the centimeter and half centimeter points along the tape. Start at zero (0). The zero mark should be at the bottom of the empty space inside the jar, not at the bottom of the glass.

3 Put the jar outside in an open space away from trees and buildings. You might like to tape it to a stake. Then wind or animals can't knock it over.

4 After each rain, write down the water level in the jar. Then empty the jar and replace it.

5 Keep a record of rainfall for several months. Your local newspaper probably reports a monthly rainfall for your area. Did you receive more or less rain than usual during the months you measured rainfall? How could you use your jar to measure rainfall in inches?

Date	Rain (cm)
Mar. 3	0.5
Mar. 9	2.25
Mar. 16	3.5
Mar. 21	0.5
Apr. 5	1.5

about 1½ cm of rain

How Much Rain Has Fallen?
The Facts

Rainfall (and snowfall) measurements help describe weather conditions. They help predict floods, droughts, and crop failures. They help people decide when to limit water use in cities and towns.

You can measure rainfall in either centimeters (cm) or inches (in). Two and one-half centimeters equal one inch. At 2.5 cm on your scale, write 1 in. Write 2 in at 5 cm.

Divide each inch into ten equal divisions. You can then record rainfall in tenths of an inch.

When snow melts, it makes liquid water. Melting snow can cause floods. Too little snow can cause a drought in some places.

Ideas for Your Science Fair

- **After a snowstorm, measure the snow's depth. Then figure out how much snowfall equals a centimeter (or inch) of rain.**

- **Suppose you put a funnel in the jar you used. The funnel is wider than the jar, so you will collect more rain. But then how would you measure the rainfall?**

- **Sound travels about 1 mile in 5 seconds. How can you use this information to find the distance to a lightning strike you see through a window?**

9

The Makings of a Cloud

Things You Will Need:

- an adult
- clear, empty, 2-liter plastic soda bottle with screw cap
- measuring cup
- warm water
- light background such as a window
- match

How do clouds form in the sky? Write down your ideas and your reasons for them.

Let's Investigate!

1 Find a clear, empty, 2-liter plastic soda bottle with a screw cap. Pour ½ cup of warm water into the bottle. Screw on the cap. Then shake the bottle.

2 Hold the bottle in front of a light background such as a window. Shake the bottle again. Then squeeze and release it. Did you see a cloud? One thing needed to make a cloud was missing.

3 Remove the cap from the bottle. **Ask an adult** to light a match, blow it out, and quickly lower the smoking match into the bottle. Smoke particles will collect inside the bottle. Quickly put the cap back on.

4 Shake the bottle again. Hold it up against a light background. Squeeze it and then suddenly release your squeeze. Did you see a cloud form this time?

In Experiment 7, you found that water vapor condenses when it cools. What else is needed to make water vapor condense and form a cloud?

squeeze   release

The Makings of a Cloud: *The Facts*

When you stopped squeezing the bottle, the pressure inside the bottle suddenly decreased. The water vapor expanded and cooled. But cooling water vapor is not enough to make a cloud. The vapor needs small particles on which to collect. There were many tiny particles in smoke that you added to the bottle. Above the ocean, the air contains salt particles. The cooling water vapor condenses on those particles, forming droplets. We see the many droplets as clouds. In real clouds, the tiny droplets often bump into one another and grow into raindrops.

Ideas for Your Science Fair

- Take photographs of clouds. How many different kinds can you identify? Which ones are likely to bring rain or snow?

- Artists often draw tear-shaped raindrops. What is the actual shape of falling raindrops? Do an experiment to find out.

Shine a flashlight into the dark by the seashore. You will see tiny salt particles.

10

Warm Air and Cool Air

Things You Will Need:

- drinking glass
- water
- empty 1-liter bottle, such as a soda bottle
- clock
- balloon
- hot tap water
- towel
- refrigerator
- freezer

What do you think happens to air when it is warmed? When it is cooled? Write down your ideas and your reasons for them.

Let's Investigate!

1 Fill a drinking glass nearly full of water. Find an empty (except for the air in it) 1-liter bottle. Turn the bottle upside down. Put the mouth of the bottle under the water in the glass.

2 Warm the air in the bottle by holding the bottle with the palms of your hands (but don't squeeze). What comes out of the bottle? Can you explain what happens?

3 Leave the bottle for 10 minutes so that air in the bottle returns to room temperature.

4 Pull the neck of a balloon over the open end of the bottle. Warm the air in the bottle by letting hot tap water flow over the bottle. What happens? How can you explain what happens?

5 Dry the bottle, and then put it in a refrigerator. After 10 minutes, look at the bottle and the attached balloon. What has happened? How can you explain what happened?

6 Put the bottle in a freezer. Predict what will happen. After 10 minutes, look at the bottle and attached balloon again. Was your prediction correct?

What does this experiment have to do with weather?

hot water

balloon

Warm Air and Cool Air: *The Facts*

You saw air expand (take up more space) when it warmed. Air bubbles came out of the bottle you held. The balloon expanded because the air in the bottle expanded when it was warmed. The balloon deflated when the air in the bottle was cooled. Because air shrinks when it cools, a liter of cold air has more air in it than a liter of warm air. A liter of cold air weighs more than a liter of warm air.

In nature, a large amount of cold air may bump into a large amount of warm air. The heavier cold air slides under the warm air. If the warm air has lots of water vapor in it, the moisture may condense and form raindrops.

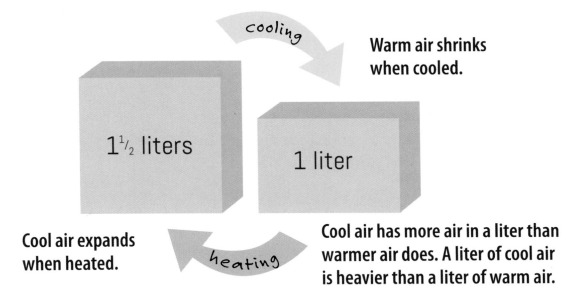

cooling

Warm air shrinks when cooled.

1½ liters

1 liter

Cool air expands when heated.

heating

Cool air has more air in a liter than warmer air does. A liter of cool air is heavier than a liter of warm air.

Ideas for Your Science Fair

- **Do liquids expand and contract when warmed or cooled? If they do, do they expand and contract the same amount and in the same way as air? Do experiments to find out.**

Glossary

air pressure The push of Earth's atmosphere, which results from the weight of air. The force presses on things from all directions: down, up, and sideways.

aneroid barometer A device that measures air pressure.

cloud A visible collection of many tiny water droplets.

condensation The change of a gas to a liquid. When water vapor (water as a gas) condenses on tiny particles in air, it forms very small droplets of water.

evaporation The change of a liquid to a gas.

expand To increase in volume (amount of space occupied). All gases, such as air, expand when heated and contract (shrink) when cooled.

temperature A measure of how hot or cold something is. It is usually measured using a thermometer with a scale divided into degrees Celsius or degrees Fahrenheit.

Tropic of Cancer An imaginary line around Earth 23.5 degrees north of the equator. It marks the sun's most northern overhead path, which occurs around June 21.

Tropic of Capricorn An imaginary line around Earth 23.5 degrees south of the equator. It marks the sun's most southern overhead path, which occurs around December 21.

water vapor Water that has become a gas.

Further Reading

Books

Ardley, Neil. *101 Great Science Experiments.* New York, NY: DK Ltd., 2014.

Buczynski, Sandy. *Designing a Winning Science Fair Project.* Ann Arbor, MI: Cherry Lake Publishing, 2014.

Latta, Sara. *All About Earth: Exploring the Planet with Science Projects.* North Mankato, MN: Capstone Press, 2016.

Margles, Samantha. *Mythbusters Science Fair Book.* New York, NY: Scholastic, 2011.

McGill, Jordan. *Earth Science Fair Projects.* New York, NY: AV² by Weigl, 2012.

Shea, Therese. *Freaky Weather Stories.* New York, NY: Gareth Stevens Publishing, 2016.

Sneideman, Joshua. *Climate Change: Discover How It Impacts Spaceship Earth.* Whiter River Junction, VT: Nomad Press, 2015.

Sohn, Emily. *Experiments in Earth Science and Weather.* North Mankato, MN: Capstone Press, 2016.

Websites

Franklin Institute
fi.edu/history-resources/weather
Explore the history of weather and weather instruments.

NASA
climatekids.nasa.gov/
Click on links and games about air, weather, water, energy, plants, and animals.

NOAA
education.noaa.gov/Weather_and_Atmosphere
Follow the links to photos and facts about the many types of weather on Earth.

Index